Revie

MW01482707

✳✳✳✳✳✳

Peter Shaffer's book about his life experience and motivation, told in the form of personal narrative, is fast moving and fascinating. His memories of growing up in our small town are right on the mark. It's an easy, entertaining read, and will help people realize how to get through life remembering what really counts.

Donovan Kramer Jr.,
Managing Editor, *Casa Grande Dispatch*

I find this Book to be a very successful formula for turning Your life around. The keen insight that Peter disburses in his Survival manual will alter your ways of thinking and reacting forever.

Joel Red Bear, M.D.
North American Indian Society for
Healthy Living (NAISHL)

Peter Shaffer writes eloquently of the triumph of the human spirit over adversity. His words of wisdom and motivational story will help every reader to grow as a person and make a difference in the world. Peter Shaffer lights you up with the glow of his internal neon and repeats the mantra—keep reassessing your life and don't give up.

Hon. Peter J. Murphy
former New Hampshire Congressman and
Women's Radio (WMEL) Talk Show Host

An exciting journey to the center of your own creative inner-being. The realty expressed within this book by Peter will empower you and drive you personally to seek the truth that you have longed to discover. That truth being, Be Yourself!

J. Fire Cloud A.I.
CEO of the North American Indian Society
for Healthy Living

After reading just the first two chapters, I related to Peter's life and seen that we all exist within similar realms of awakening. This is a powerful study and a very useful tool to use for finding your inner true path.

Jacob Blue Feather M.A.
Co-Founder/CTO of Blue Feather Film Productions Ltd.
Phoenix Rising Experience 1968-?

Shaffer's journey from unhappiness to self-realization may help guide readers who are dissatisfied with their working lives but who don't know why, or what to do about their emotional paralysis. He outlines his own explorations, some of which took great courage to begin. He's certainly a motivator!"

Peter Guinta,
Senior Writer, *St. Augustine Record*

Motivation for Survival

Motivation for Survival

Peter Shaffer

INFINITY
PUBLISHING.COM

ISBN 0-7414-5798-9
First Edition

Published by:

PUBLISHING.COM

1094 New DeHaven Street, Suite 100
West Conshohocken, PA 19428-2713
Info@buybooksontheweb.com
www.buybooksontheweb.com
Toll-free (877) BUY BOOK
Local Phone (610) 941-9999
Fax (610) 941-9959

Printed in the United States of America

Published January 2010

This book is dedicated to my wife Rebecca

and daughter Ashley

Acknowledgments

******

For this book I want to particularly thank my wife, Rebecca. Not only was she the inspiration for my life's journey, she inspires me daily to be my very best. I wake up every day knowing how lucky I am to be married to her.

My daughter Ashley, who I am very proud of, continues to always surprise me with her accomplishments. She truly is a miracle and a joy in my life. I, like other fathers, am making this effort for *them*.

I want to thank my friend Peter who motivated me five years ago to write a book. He told me, "You can do it", and "It's not that hard". I didn't listen at first, but he kept asking, "How's your book coming," and I finally listened. Peter motivated me to make this book possible.

My family, friends and life experiences continue to MOTIVATE my LIFE for SURVIVAL, and I hope you use this sharing from my heart. If you do, you will find success and enjoyment in all your future endeavors.

Table of Contents

******

Author's Note

✳✳✳✳✳✳

All the information contained in this book has been written to help illustrate a major closing point. All incidents, situations, and objects depicted in this book are based on the author's own experiences and writings.

It is the sincere hope of the author that the lessons learned from this book are beneficial, not only to the reader's future, but to his or her undying spirit.

Chapter 1
What Are You Doing Here?

******

I remember waking up one morning and saying to myself, "What am I doing here?" I had these thoughts before, but I never acted upon them until that day in April.

I had been married for 15 years, divorced for five years and was living in Melbourne, Florida. My ex lived about a quarter mile away with my daughter who was 16. I visited Ashley on the weekends and always tried to do something athletic with her. We hit baseballs at the batting cage, played tennis, went turtle watching and walked on the beach when it wasn't too hot. I was called the "fun dad". I tried to get her senses going and encouraged her mind to explore and dream with sensory movements. What fun it is to teach someone to think beyond the old humdrum of life. You can get yourself in a RUT quickly if you don't keep your mind active and exercise your body. I bet you have heard that before haven't you? It's time to begin your journey of becoming motivated. You will become super-positive about life; no matter whether times are good or bad. You will survive!

Hurricanes were happening all the time during the Katrina years in Florida. I lost my fence and lost my roof. I became sick of the heat, bugs, and humidity. When you lose power in Florida in the middle of the summer for eight days, with 90 plus degree temperatures, you are miserable!

People count on electricity and are really angry when they don't have food or ice. I saw suffering, despair, and people in lines getting food and ice from FEMA, from churches and from the Salvation Army. I saw people lose businesses, savings, and respect for law enforcement. Thieves were very busy!

I struggled against losing my self-respect. I can't say it was all bad. It just wasn't for me! At that time I had been selling industrial chemicals for five years, traveling a thousand miles a week throughout Florida. The driving was getting to me, but I was able to daydream trying not to fall asleep on I-95. I finally decided to quit because I was BURNT OUT! Always remember, you're not a quitter if you have tried giving it your all.

Real estate was going crazy at that time. People were buying houses and flipping them. Florida was becoming an overpriced market, and the buying frenzy kept going. People were even buying homes that weren't finished and those that had hurricane damage.

I decided to take a week off from chemicals and went to real estate school to get my license. As I sat in the class of 400 students, I realized the instructor was making big bucks at $425 per person in the class.

I studied pretty hard for the real estate exam and drove 100 miles to take the test. I failed! I didn't quit and took it again. I failed! The third time, I got refresher training and failed again. Keep in mind each time you take the test it costs TIME AND MONEY. At that time, it was about $50 per test to retake the exam.

After failing the fourth time, I said, "Real estate isn't for me!" I threw the books in a corner and concentrated on my chemical job, but I still saw a lot of people getting rich in real estate. And I was still driving those 1,000 miles a week. I finally told myself that I needed a CHANGE. I decided to give my two-weeks' notice, and bought a business.

My boss was shocked! He flew in from North Carolina, worked with me a couple of days, and learned what needed to be done. Those two weeks was very uncomfortable for me. Usually when you move to another job, it is uncomfortable. However, I knew, for ME to become stronger and a better person, I had to MAKE A MOVE.

I figured something fun would be the ticket to my success. I bought a tanning salon about ten miles from the beach called Hot Bunz in Palm Bay, Florida. I thought it was a pretty cool name. I shook my head every day when approximately 50 clients came to the salon to get a tan. I met a lot of nice people and realized they were there to "feel good."

The clients were doing something for themselves to RECHARGE their batteries. I was working very hard day and night. If you've ever owned a business, you understand. I saw many businesses come and go at the strip mall where I was located. Most owners blamed the economy, the competition; the cloudy skies, and whatever else they could think of. I must have heard a thousand reasons why business was slow.

My business was between a barbershop and a beauty salon. One day I was sitting outside the salon waiting for the next customer to come in. This hairdresser told me, "No matter how bad your business is, never tell anybody."

What a revelation that was! I thought to myself, people don't want to hear negative talk! Personally, I wasn't saying anything bad to anybody, but other owners were. They were consumed with negativity. As a customer, when you walk in a store, do you want to hear about the horrible economy, or the rain, or anything NEGATIVE? NO WAY!

Customers want to be sold and be happy with their purchase. They want to *feel good* about their decision to buy. Customers are looking for a great shopping experience!

Never ever talk negative. Read this again. NEVER EVER, TALK NEGATIVE! One more time, NEVER TALK NEGATIVE!

Life was going pretty good at the tanning salon until three competitors moved in within two miles of the store. My business started going south. I worked even harder to regain customers who were "trying out" the new salons. They left me for about three months and eventually came back.

I was struggling and finally by listening to a few friends, Fire Cloud, Billy and Peter, I kept going at a POSITIVE and fast-paced rate. I turned it around by advertising, cutting prices and then it finally hit me. I never, ever, talked negative about the competition. My competitors did and it ruined them in the long run. One of the "new" salons closed down in three months.

Several business owners would tell the customers, business was "slow" when they asked "How's business?" As a customer, how does that make you feel? Do you think less of that company? Do you instantly think of going to another store? Do you find that kind of talk NEGATIVE? You're darn right you do! You don't want to hear that.

Suddenly, it hit me like an earthquake. It took me 15 years to figure it out! I wasn't happy in Melbourne and needed to move on! I didn't want to fail. My motivation to survive kicked in. I knew this business was killing me, and I had to sell it for my sanity.

Sometimes in life, you get hit with a big stick and your mind comes alive again. I wish somebody had hit me much sooner! I didn't LISTEN TO MY GUT that told me it's time to make a change. I was stubborn. When I listened, my life has changed.

Hurricanes were continual during the "Katrina years". I was getting killed in business because electricity was out for more than a week. I needed power to run the beds. I made a decision to sell the business. It took almost nine months to sell it. I decided I was going to leave Melbourne, and I put my house up for sale. Real estate was hot at the time, and I sold it within a month for a good profit. I traveled to Tampa to Lazy Dayz RV dealership and bought an RV, a travel trailer. It was a brand new Coachman 21-foot model. I was so excited and asked the salesperson to store the trailer until I closed on my house.

As I go along telling my motivational story, you might notice I refer to my *Journey*. When I say *Journey*, it is the eight month trip I took by myself with my RV traveling the "good old USA." It was the trip of my lifetime and completely turned my thinking around and helped me "find myself."

After traveling the United States starting out in Florida, I landed in San Diego, California. I passed my Real Estate exam the first time and got a job at a prestigious Real Estate company in La Jolla. The first house I sold was three million!

This was going great until the recession hit and my wife and I decided to move to Hawaii after visiting there on our honeymoon. I passed the Hawaii Real Estate Exam the first time also.

Oh by the way—PAY ATTENTION TO THE UPPER CASE WORDS. They will be your guides to success in your future. These words hopefully will motivate all your efforts.

Chapter 2
Small-town Values

******

I will come back to telling you about my experiences in Florida, but now I want to tell you about my youth. I grew up in a small town called Casa Grande, Arizona. It is the hot spot of the nation during the summer months. Temperatures up to 120 degrees are not uncommon. It was nice, but extremely hot! I was the youngest of five with three brothers and my sister. My father sold Case tractors. He worked very hard and was the breadwinner for the family. He stuck with that job for 20 years. My mother stayed home and took very good care of us kids. When we came home from school, she was always there waiting for us, a value long forgotten in today's high-paced two-family member working society. When we came home, she was there to make us do our chores and finish our homework.

My mother instilled religion in us, and we went to church every Sunday rain or shine. Having good VALUES and maintaining the family unit were very important to my parents. I strongly recommend it to you.

No matter what your faith is, just go to church! I strongly feel going to church every week not only instills a REGIMEN, but from my experience it helped me to remember that I didn't have it so bad and to reflect on the happiness I had experienced during the week. My father didn't go to church, but he drove us there each week. Think about it. Do you really have it so bad?

We lived in a small three-bedroom two-bath house. It didn't seem to matter for me, but we were really cramped in the small house. I never noticed that we weren't rich. I didn't know any other way to live. I held several part-time jobs before I was 16 including being a paperboy, lawn boy and third-shift manager (the person who closed and cleaned up at night) at a fast food restaurant called Whataburger. Pretty funny name, huh?

My mother was very strict. She and my dad were instrumental in helping all of us boys become Eagle Scouts. At one time, we had the Arizona state record for the most Eagle Scouts in one family. All of my siblings' first names start with a "P" and we have no middle names. My sister Patty was the first college graduate. She went to the University of Arizona and became a registered nurse. This was huge in our family! My oldest brother Phil joined the Navy, met his wife in France and moved there. He got out of the small town! My middle brother Patrick graduated from the U.S. Air Force Academy in Colorado Springs, and my brother Paul became a special education teacher.

My mother wanted all of us to learn how to swim. She took us to the American Red Cross swimming lessons in the summer. I remember sticking my tongue out at her for making me blow bubbles. I also remember hating to study and bringing home average grades. My mother was tough with all of us. She had the desire to help us SUCCEED! She was one of those people you hear about who graduated from college, walked five miles through the snow and didn't eat a lot during the struggle.

Since my mother went to college, WE ALL WERE GOING TO COLLEGE! It was extremely important to her that we not only went to college but graduated! She made it her GOAL.

She was my foundation for goal setting. I just realized that now as I am writing this book. Goal setting is important! How many times have you heard that? How may times have you written your goals down on paper? Ninety percent of the people have never written down their goal.

I was one of the 90 percent until a good friend asked me point blank, "Did you write goals down?" When I finally did, two years after he was successful writing them down, I became extremely successful. Stop right now and take three minutes to write (on paper) ten goals for the next three months. You must work on this right now! Stop everything you are doing, and write them NOW. Don't STOP, write them now! TURN OFF THE NOISE AND WRITE THEM DOWN!

Did you do it? It wasn't that hard, was it? I'll bet it was easier than you thought. Goal setting is an ongoing exercise. If you're a procrastinator, you must define each goal with a specific completion date. You say to yourself, "On Monday I will do this. On Tuesday I will do this, and so on. Never quit. MEASUREMENT of success is finding out if you did it and did it well!

Some people can get a task done before the "designated self completion date." I congratulate them and all the more power to them. Have you ever noticed not completing your goals until the last day? GOALS ARE MENTAL. If your mind is POSITIVE each and every day, then you will complete your goals faster. Remember this.

Chapter 3
Become Positive

******

By now you have written your goals. Congratulations! This may be the first time you ever did it. You should be proud of yourself; you have taken the first step to SUCCESS.

Most of my motivational writing in this book came from observing other people and being OUTSIDE. Motivation comes from exercise, sunny days, good weather, and clear thoughts in your mind. It also comes from bad things that have happened in the past: losing a "big" sale or losing a competition.

In either case, motivation will not come unless you are aware of your surroundings, for example, getting outside and observing nature. I find when you are walking down a hallway or sidewalk, it is very motivating if you simply LOOK UP.

Do you remember when people told you to "keep you head up" or say "chin up"? Have you ever simply looked up at the sky and noticed the clouds, birds, trees or the movement of the wind?

Your posture improves when you become positive and keep your head up. Crunching down and looking down lowers your confidence. Confidence is quickly raised when you look at the bright side or become positive and not let the outside influences affect your being.

I am sitting poolside at the Illikaki Hotel next to a couple in Hawaii. A lady is talking on her cell phone. She looks about 65 but probably is 45. She hasn't been taking care of herself and seems to be a busybody. I normally don't eavesdrop on people, but the pool isn't crowded and I can't help hearing.

As she is talking on the phone, only negative statements come out of her mouth. She says, "I'm going to take a couple of allergy pills tonight and they will knock me out." She was asking her daughter when she was going to have the operation and how she was feeling. She asked her, "Are you sure?" and "Are you getting enough sleep?" and "Are you feeling all right?"

She told her she didn't like this and she didn't like that. She talked about the weather. She said, "It rained yesterday and it better not rain today. I don't like the rain and I'm not getting enough color in the sun." You get the idea! She was totally negative. Why does it have to be this way? It doesn't! It will bring YOU down in a second if you let it. She is a "victim" of circumstances. She has a negative streak that needs to change to positive.

Her husband was the same way and complained all day. Most of the hour or so, he was on the phone and not enjoying the perfect 75 degree, sunny day.

If everybody were as bad off as they are, nothing would get done in this country. We would all feel sorry for ourselves! Why do you suppose some people are totally negative and others are positive, can work with others, exude confidence and know how to get the job done? Maybe it's because they want to become the best at their craft. Maybe they don't let anything or anyone spoil the dreams. Are you this way?

Are you that positive, dynamic person? Are you a winner, motivator and all-around great person to be with? If not, can you change your attitude? You bet you can. It's all about your attributes to win, succeed and not let anything stop you from completing your dreams.

Remember when I was talking about becoming POSITIVE? You must immediately strive to become positive. Don't worry if you are not. It took me 40 years to become what I call POSITIVE. Hopefully, your positive attitude will come much faster than it did for me.

Do you remember your "formative years"? My formative years stopped one afternoon very suddenly. My life was changed and I faced a tremendous struggle. I became a better man for it.

My father had made his biggest tractor sale of his life. He was driving back home after selling three Case tractors. The commission was going to be huge! You see, my dad started his career in Casa Grande as a parts manager for Norm Bingham Tractor and Equipment Company. The farm implement company sold tractors to clear land and pick cotton. He rose to the top of the company and was asked to sell tractors when the sales rep retired.

My father never took a sales course in his life but knew every farmer in the area because they had to come to him to buy the parts. His RAPPORT with the CUSTOMER was all about TRUST. They all liked him, and so they bought from him! Have you every heard this? Have you ever purchased something and didn't like the salesperson? Probably not! If a customer likes you, your percentage is higher in selling them a product.

Becoming likeable is extremely important. That goes for everything in life! Sugar is better than coal when it comes to interaction with people. Remember this and you will become a POSITIVE person. Why do you suppose this is true? Maybe because you get what you want out of life if you're more positive. Isn't that important to you? You know it is!

Back to my life experience at the age of 16. As I said, my father made his biggest sale on a hot spring day. While he was driving home in the desert, a school bus was stopped along the cotton fields, and my father was traveling very fast. He noticed a child running in front of the bus and swerved to miss him. He crashed into the back of the school bus. He was pinned in the car and a helicopter flew him to the hospital. He was in intensive care in Phoenix at Good Samaritan Hospital about 50 miles away for eight long days.

The doctor said he probably wouldn't walk again. I remember all of the tubes hooked up to him. My mother was a basket case and traveled 50 miles each way every day to the hospital. She didn't have the money to stay in a hotel and drove home each night.

About two o'clock one morning—it happened! We were called to come into the hospital. My father had suffered a pulmonary aneurysm and was on life support. My mother and I rushed to the hospital. He was still alive, and we called all my siblings to travel in and see him. He died the next day.

I remember somebody asking, "What's Peter going to do?" My brothers and sister were afraid for both my mom and me. I cried a whole bunch but tried to be strong for my mother. I took care of her the best I knew how. She MOTIVATED me to become strong and help her. We used each other's strength to heal our wounds.

We had the funeral at St Anthony's Catholic Church and buried him at the desert cemetery. My father had taken care of everything in the funeral, but he didn't have a will. The bad news: here comes probate for two years! GET A WILL! Call an attorney right now, and get it DONE.

Well, there I was with all the greatest love in the world from my parents and family, and my life was in total shambles. I became particularly sad, because my father never got to see all my accomplishments! It was DEPRESSING! I trained myself to be tough and FILL THE SADNESS with a BETTER DAY the NEXT DAY. They all say, "Let it go". That's easy to say!

I became an Eagle Scout, was in the barbershop quartet at Casa Grande Union High School, passed the physical agility test, became a part-time firefighter and started going to community college. I was depressed because my father never saw my strengths become reality. I ended up rationalizing the sadness away and kept moving forward. Always MOVE FORWARD and keep your motivation going. NEVER QUIT! I know you have heard that before. If you haven't, where have you been?

I was sad, depressed and wondered why this happened to me. But I overcame, which wasn't easy and kept on striving for something better. I had to be stronger to support my mother in her grief. I was the man of the house now and had to help take care of everything. I grew up quickly, like so many other kids under the same circumstances.

The old saying, "Never judge another man until you walk in his shoes" is absolutely true. Seeing other people get through life struggles is a POSITIVE INFLUENCE. Sometimes when we observe others who are going through tough times, we can learn a way to control our own negative influences. Therefore, always OBSERVE things: other people and nature. You will become grounded and influenced by outside energy forces. "Stop and smell the roses."

By helping my mother, I became stronger at dealing with life's challenges. I learned how to clean and repair the house the quick way. She really depended on me, but I was just "ok" in school as far as getting good grades -- nothing to write home about.

When my father died, I was failing a high school history class. School was about to let out and I missed taking my final exam because I was at the hospital with my dad. I will never forget coming to my teacher asking to take the exam. He said, "Don't worry about it," and let me skip the exam. He also gave me a C on my report card for the class. I didn't know it at the time, but he was renting a house right around the corner from my house in the same neighborhood. He knew the whole story about my dad. The town was small

18

with a population of about 15,000. The newspaper told the story very well about my dad and his accident. Everybody loved Jake. We all need a break in life. Be thankful when you get it!

You may think I was lucky not having to take the final, but it wasn't luck. It was circumstance. Life is nothing but circumstances that cause a reaction. To achieve the right reaction, we must become motivational and positive. Have a purpose! You've heard all this before, now haven't you? Well *listen* this time! It may just help.

My father missed so many accomplishments. I raised the bicentennial flag on July 4, 1976, in front of Casa Grande Union High School. I won an award for newspaper carrier of the month, at the "Casa Grande Dispatch." I won merit badges in Boy Scouts.

I missed my father's stories and the way he taught me to fix the car, work with my hands and mind my manners. I feel if you grow up in a stable environment, you will become successful. Have you heard that before? Sometimes exploring the history and past accomplishments of leaders sheds light on your ability to become a winner.

It came time to go to college! My mother motivated me at an early age to do just that. It's almost like she brainwashed me into visualizing myself graduating and becoming somebody. She motivated me to be a free thinker with boundaries and core values like going to church every Sunday, no cussing, coming home when school lets out and being on time. You have heard all of these things haven't you. Are you doing them? Start now, if you aren't.

At that time, there was a man who owned a waste management business. It was a "new thing" at the time. I was very interested in the plastic boxes and the pumping of the *"sludge through to the sugar truck."* You get the idea.

The business was for sale, and I wanted to blow off college and buy that business. My third brother told me, "You're going to college." I should have, could have bought it and made a great living today, but I was motivated by outside influences to "go to college". Why do you suppose they wanted me to go?

My brother Patrick who went to the U.S. Air Force Academy and my mother told me "You're going to college." He also was the one who talked me out of going into business.

He did it to make my life better. I am very glad he did. I needed advice from a "father figure" at that time.

Chapter 4
Going to College

******

I drove to Central Arizona College (CAC) about 15 miles away to get the basics out of the way. The campus was very peaceful and situated in the desert. I tried hard to succeed! English wasn't my greatest subject. I literally had a party for myself when I finished my second year of English. I told myself I would never use English again! I was dead wrong! This book is based on a great invention called "spell check".

I learned how to interact with other personalities and minds, and I captured some great educational stimuli. I worked in audiovisual and ran the "sound" board in the auditorium. I enjoyed the job and met several entertainers.

I was motivated to graduate, and my brothers and sisters were constantly checking in on me to see if I was doing OK. I was doing OK and my mother was getting stronger each day.

After community college and GRADUATING with an Associates of Science degree, I went to Northern Arizona University (NAU) in Flagstaff, Arizona. Now, NAU was the big-time school where kids made it or failed. I was scared to death, not of the school that sat at 7,000 feet elevation in the mountains, but the indecision of what to major in.

I literally went to registration, looked at the big signs that said English Department, Math Department and choose the Psychology department. I thought it would be interesting and easy. Interesting it was, but easy it was not! I was away from home for the first time in my life and living in a dormitory. I was nervous and told myself to be cool to get along. My peers must accept me or I wouldn't survive. I also had to "buckle down" and study to graduate!

My brother Paul motivated me to pick NAU because he graduated from there. He and I drove up (three hours away) to look around and check out the campus. He stayed in the dorm called Tinsley Hall and we visited his old room. It was a beautiful campus in the mountains. The pine trees were huge!

I applied for the Tinsley Hall dormitory and got it! My residence manager's name was Jack. He had a tough-guy demeanor, and so I acted cool so I could FIT IN. Fitting in is extremely important in the beginning especially with a new job.

I used my determined calmness to fit in. I decided it was necessary to FIT IN FIRST. After I was able to be one of the guys, I could let my personality loose. All in all, I was accepted in college and felt bad for those who weren't.

On the first day of my arrival, I will never forget that Jack noticed my new hiking books. I purchased them for $80, a great deal of money back then. He said, "It's going to take you a long time to break those boots in. You better put some SNOW SEAL on them so they won't leak in the snow." The tone of Jack's voice was to always BE PREPARED and TAKE CHARGE!

I studied pretty hard and played very hard. I went fishing with Mark and John for Northern Pike. We had fun playing football in the snow and went skiing at Snow Bowl ski resort.

I joined Air Force Reserve Officer Training Course (ROTC) and sort of followed my brother's footsteps. I decided I was going to join the Air Force.

I didn't like the marching exercises in R.O.T.C every Friday, but GRADUATED from college with a Bachelor's in Psychology and became a 2nd Lieutenant in the Air Force. I was an officer! Wow!

My whole family surprised me and came to my graduation. One brother said he couldn't believe I was going to graduate. He said the reason he showed up to see it for himself!

I wasn't that bad, but he was funny then and still is today. Life's all about GRADUATION and finishing your GOALS. You must GRADUATE every day to become successful and never ever quit even if you have no money. NEVER QUIT—NEVER!

Steps to Motivation

Read this several times in the month and work on each step.

Remember you were programmed when you were born and during your upbringing for good or bad. Reprogram your mind in the morning and night using these words and phases. Use phrases like "I am a winner, I like myself, I am going to be successful by this day and time this week, I am a great person, My life is changing each day."

Think Positive

Exercise, exercise and then exercise again.

Get out of the house and breathe fresh air.

Limit TV to 1 hour per day.

Stop the noise.

GO	**G**
OUT	**O**
AND	**A**
LIGHT	**L**
STICKS	**S**

What do I mean by "go out and light sticks?" Well, that spells GOALS. By setting goals, you keep your FIRE AND DESIRE burning. Without sticks added to a fire, the fire will go out. You must always keep your internal fire burning with a strong desire to become the best.

Sticks are added by your desire to make changes. By having an absolutely positive attitude combined with a roadmap, you will greatly increase the chances of life's best things happening.

I strongly believe in goal setting. You must have GOALS WRITTEN. Remember this from Chapter 1. STOP reading and start writing now or you will never accomplish what you want out of life. Your goals must be clear and well written.

Always, always strive to think positive.

Pick you battles and sell yourself all the time.

Wear nice clothes and watch out for bad habits like drinking and smoking. Walk fast!

Write 10 places you want to go right now. Place a date of completion for each task on the paper. Look at that list every night.

Write down 10 things you want to accomplish in the next six months. These must be obtainable rather than pie in the sky. Look at the list in the morning and at night before you go to bed. Write it down NOW! Try it, and you will find it works. If you don't complete these 10 goals in six months, send me an email. Will you always write down your goals? Will you COMMIT to writing your goals down?

Believe in yourself and become active in your community. When you write your GOALS, put on paper exactly what you expect and what the outcome will be. Eliminate mistakes and get better every week. Find your passion, do it well, and treat everybody right.

You become what you think most of the time. Visualize where you want to go and get there! Never let anything stop you!

Chapter 5

The Graduate and Air Force Officer

******

Peter is big time now! He has gold bars on his shoulder, met a girl to marry and graduated from college with a Bachelors Degree. All his MOTIVATIVING FACTORS are in place and he is successful!

I accomplished my goal, listened to the motivators in my life and worked hard to achieve the goal of graduating. I patted myself on the back at least one time. I got married before I went to training in California. After training, I took my new wife and was stationed at F.E. Warren Air Force base in Cheyenne, Wyoming.

Cheyenne was COLD! It was a nice western town with great people but COLD and WINDY! The people were very strong due to the conditions and climate. They said if you lived in Cheyenne and the wind stopped, you would fall over. I believed it. The temperature was 30 below on several occasions. This is without the wind chill factor.

I worked as an executive officer in a security police squadron. I was commanded by Major "D". What a tough $*$ (use nice words Peter; this is a family book) to work for. I was only 22, blond with blue eyes, skinny and nerdy. I couldn't wait to look old. I was in charge of people twice my age. I figured out quickly how to lead them by LISTENING. My motivation was to be liked and become respected. I learned fast what NOT to say if you wanted somebody to do something for you.

If I needed something done, I would ask the senior enlisted members with questions like, "Do you think we could do it like this?" Or "Do you think we can get that done by Friday?" I tried never to say, "Do this" or "Do that". It doesn't go over well. I made more honey by asking and not telling.

A lot of officers didn't learn this valuable lesson and eventually were dismissed by their own accord. I was young, stupid and did what I was told. The administrators who worked for me kept me out of trouble by politely saying, "Lieutenant, you may want to do it this way."

COMMUNICATION in the beginning got me in trouble and kept me out of trouble when I learned the valuable lesson of LISTENING. I will never forget an old master sergeant who in private told me one day, "Lieutenant, use this before you use this." He was pointing at his brain and then his mouth. I learned that lesson quick!

While I was in Cheyenne, I wanted to be reassigned to Alaska, a hard base to get. I successfully got an assignment to Elmendorf Air Force Base in Anchorage Alaska. People I spoke with couldn't believe an Arizona boy was going to Alaska. They were very envious.

When I arrived on base, I was supposed to be an executive officer for a fighter squadron. I was diverted to a little known job called "protocol". UGH!

In protocol, I was helping all the dignitaries and generals who came on the base. This was the worst job of my life! I had no life! I literally worked six weeks straight without a day off. There was a master sergeant who worked alongside me taking Rolaids everyday. The stress was incredible.

Because my back kept going out I went to the base doctor. I told him my back hurt and asked for some pain pills. He sent me down to physical therapy to teach me how to exercise my back. I didn't get any pain pills. I was stressed out and very out of shape! I have blocked most of this job from memory.

When I did have a day off, I tried my hand at salmon fishing. I caught a few big ones. We traveled and saw some huge icebergs. Alaska has some of the most beautiful scenery in the world.

One day the author James Michener came to the base and I met him. He was visiting Alaska to write the book *Alaska*. The general on the base gave him a briefing and a grand tour of the base. He also flew him up to Danali National Park.

Mr Michener was treated like royalty. He got the best tour from us, and learned everything he could about Alaska. I really admired his easy-going demeanor and knew one day I would become a writer.

One day, my wife fell on her hip and needed another artificial hip transplant. The Air Force flew both of us to her orthopedic surgeon at the University of Arizona in Tucson for the operation. She got a new hip transplant and recuperated at my mom's house in Casa Grande. It was very nice visiting my mother. I helped her around the house until we could travel back.

When we came back, and with my PERSISTANCE, the Air Force decided they didn't have the medical facilities to take care of her in Alaska. We got a humanitarian reassignment to Keesler Air Force Base in Biloxi, Mississippi.

I loved the Cajun food in Biloxi and the southern hospitality. I loved to fish, catch crab and eat all the shrimp and seafood I could find. I ate Poboys, fried catfish and mullet. I ate so much good food and remember eating more crawfish at a party than three people. Biloxi is named

"Hurricane Alley" after several devastating storms destroyed the town. There were two in the four years I was there.

A very good friend was Bill Schoen and his wife Betty. Bill was a Cajun from New Orleans and owned a house on a canal in Ocean Springs, Mississippi. Bill was a total CAN DO, NEVER QUIT, kind of guy. He was my student training advisor along with Ron Sliga my First Sergeant at the 3413 Student Squadron. I was the commander of this squadron with 500 members straight out of basic training.

These were teenagers who were temporarily assigned to Keesler to learn their new career. Peter was a Commander now. Wow! He's big-time!

One day, Bill Schoen came to work and both of his hands were swollen and bruised. I asked him what happened. He said, "I roofed my house over the weekend." Now, this house wasn't small. It was about 2,500 square feet.

Bill roofed the entire place by himself on the weekend. You talk about a hard worker! He didn't like wasting money, and fixed things himself if he could. He OVERCAME the PAIN and his determination finished the task.

Have you ever met somebody who could do everything, someone who can fix or make anything? The kind of "go to" person who is a great friend you can trust. If I ever needed help, Bill and Betty were there for me.

A good friend will help you move. People usually run fast when you say you're moving. A good friend will help you along the way and give good advice. FIND A FRIEND you can count on, one who will help you when you need to bounce around solutions to a problem.

About a year after we arrived in Biloxi TRADEGY STRIKES! My wife had several health problems. She was constantly in and out of the hospital. The doctors told us not to have children. We didn't listen. It seemed we wanted a child so badly that we decided to take the risk. After trying on our own, we went to a fertility doctor who prescribed a drug called Clomid.

My son, Thomas Jacob, was born two months early and died a day after birth. This is the shortened version of how it transpired. I had a difficult time writing this chapter as you might imagine.

The funeral was at the graveside at the Veterans Cemetery in Biloxi. Several Air Force members, commanders, and families attend. People were shocked, and depression set in for both of us. I think about the baby often.

About three months later, I was riding with a sergeant who said his wife was a social worker for Catholic Social Services. She helped people with adoption. I firmly believe God sent her to me. We both visited the social worker and nearly two years later, we were called to pick up our baby. We named her Ashley Louise. What a fantastic day that was!

I was like a kid in the candy shop with Ashley. She is so beautiful and was spoiled by the grandparents and by us. She was an angel from heaven.

Now RESPONSIBILITY takes a huge role in my life. It was up to me to feed another mouth! I worked very hard and did my best and made it happen.

I remembered having a party when my daughter was potty trained and I didn't have to buy diapers anymore. The second party I had was when she stopped eating baby food and turned to real food! I probably partied for the wrong reasons, but that was a great accomplishment in my "breadwinner" mentality. With each step, I was saving money.

Ashley grew up like most kids. She was happy, had some great friends and really liked to be outside. She is the love of my life and I treasure the time we spend together.

This chapter and the events that happened are shortened. I can't tell you how hard it was to write this chapter. Life is quick and decisive. My point is spend every minute of the day enjoying what you have. SPEND LIFE TO THE FULLEST.

Chapter 6
Pick Your Battles

******

Everybody in a relationship fights. I don't care if you think "They are the nicest couple" they still argue. They may say they never fight, but don't believe it. It is extremely important to be careful what you say. Words cannot be taken back.

Sometimes the challenges of life cause us to argue. We all have our problems, but a winner figures how to solve them. Are you a winner? You bet you are!

Take time to remember what happened the last time you argued. Can you remember what you were fighting about? I bet you can't. Do you think it was important to fight about? It may have been at the time, but was it worth it? Why waste your time? If you can curb your aggression and find solutions, I can guarantee you will feel a whole lot better in the long run. Fighting and name-calling waste time.

Sometimes, we all mentally are down and take our aggressions out on the person we love. Don't do it! If it does happen, make up fast! Let me repeat, "MAKE UP FAST!"

Holding a grudge does nothing but prolong the anger. Do you really need to be right all the time? Is it necessary to be the winner? Do you realize how much negative time and energy you waste by fighting? Get over it, make up and get on with your goals, aspirations and fantastic motivating self!

Steps to Remember

Listen with your ears and mind. Stop for two seconds (COUNT THEM) before you respond to a question. In that way you can determine if you want to answer a question with a question or simply say yes or no.

Leave work at work. Try not to bring work home if humanly possible. Don't bring your BAGGAGE HOME on a bad day at work. Your loved ones will squash you! They don't want to hear it!

When I was selling copy machines, I found the largest oak tree in Melbourne and dumped all my worries on that tree as I was driving home each night. It worked. I felt a great relief when I did. Find a WORRY TREE and let stress leave you, before you walk in that door.

Watch the alcohol, eat right and get enough sleep. If you're FAT, seek help from a trainer. Stop saying, "I need to lose weight." Start doing and get some help if you're not motivated to complete the task by yourself.

Excessive drinking is a brain stopper. Watch it and don't drink to excess. Hangovers are never your friend and neither is a DUI.

You must eat correctly and stay away from germs by washing your hands often. A healthy athlete is effective. Become an athlete and walk fast when you walk.

Seek love and love your passion. Never, ever quit, never. Even if you have no money—never, ever quit. Seek help from a psychiatrist or psychologist or MD for life planning or goal setting, if this book doesn't give you all you need.

Wasting time by arguing is nonproductive. Learn from your mistakes, develop habits that provide results not failures and be careful not to bring your worries home.

The quality of work you do is very important to your livelihood. Don't be an idiot and always complain about your job. If you don't like the work, get out and find something better. Your boss doesn't want to hear your complaints!

If you choose the right time and the right place to confront your boss, you will be successful. You better have all your ducks in line if you want to complain. Make sure you're prepared to win the battle and accomplish your goal for change. The boss will respect you more if you are prepared. If you have a better plan, present it, but discuss the problem and solution at the right time.

Chapter 7
Seek Stress Relief

✷✷✷✷✷✷

Seek mental stimuli. What I mean by that is go to the library, to a community park or to an art gallery. Paint and clean your house or apartment. Visit a hospital and volunteer. Window-shop and smell the flowers. See and hear moving water like a waterfall or fountain. It calms you down every single time. Stop and find quiet. Go in a dark room and close your eyes and feel the calmness. It will help you to re-center.

Stress relief doesn't mean smoking or drinking heavily to let your problems go away. It means facing the problem head-on. The faster you solve it, the faster your stress goes away. That's what stress relief is all about.

Sometimes we worry about stupid things that we think are going to happen. Some people worry about what's happening at work on Monday. Your mind plays tricks on you to think you're going to get chewed out by your boss because you didn't finish the project. Or you think, "My boss is coming back from his vacation and will be piling work on me." Is it worth your valuable time not to enjoy your time off? Why waste time not recharging yourself, worrying about what's to come on Monday? You will be able to OVERCOME stress. Don't let it control your life.

Steps to Remember

POUND	**P**
OUT	**O**
WORRIES	**W**
	POW!

Don't worry. It always gets better. Time will change thing. Just become POSITIVE. If you let them get to you, they will own you. Give all your problems the big POW!

I remember in college I took a stress management class. The teacher told us to place our heads on the desk and close our eyes. He turned off the lights. We were taught to start with your toes, tense all the muscles in your body, and relax. He slowly started by talking quietly and had us tense are entire body. I will never forget the guy who fell fast asleep and was snoring very loudly! That was funny. I do this exercise often, and I have learned to use only the muscles required for any activity, thus reducing muscle stress.

What do you really like to do? If you absolutely love your job or hobby, your stress will decrease. Do you like to work with your hands, surf, play baseball or go butterfly hunting? If you do one of these activities, your stress will go away. Think and play hard and don't just sit in a chair!

Step outside of yourself and see the real you. Be another person for a minute. See if you really like what that person is doing. If you don't, try reprogramming yourself.

If you have a setback, try to fix it fast. Troubled relationships, fighting, money and addictions cause stress. A setback is nothing more than a setup for better things to happen! Find a quiet place and dream of better things to come if you can!

Steps to Remember

POUND	P
OUT	O
EVERY	E
MISTAKE	M

POEM!

Make your life a POEM. You need to figure out what mistakes you made, write them down, and fix them like a beautiful POEM. Pound out every mistake and find solutions, improve and be the best you can be.

Finding a low stress place to unwind is very hard these days. You are bombarded with traffic noise, overcrowding, high buildings and bad weather. If you SEEK QUIET PLACES your body will refresh itself. If you go and reflect at churches, parks, or museums, your body rebuilds itself.

As I was traveling on my "Journey" I used my laptop to stay connected. I emailed pictures of my trip, and everybody was excited for me. Sometimes the people I spoke with were jealous. I can understand that emotion, and it is to be avoided because it wastes time and energy.

When you get caught up in routine or are under a lot of stress, you wish you were some place else. Remember to always STAY CONNECTED with clients and family members. They may be the best advisers you have. They can help you attack your stress and correct the problems that are consuming your life.

Even world leaders don't work 24 hours a day. They take vacations. Doing nothing is an exhilarating feeling! Do it! Reflex and rebuild your mind and spirit. It works wonders for the soul.

I remember during my RV trip, I was completely stressed out for three weeks. I left Melbourne and couldn't relax. My mind was preoccupied on what I had done. I left everything, sold my house and my business. I didn't have a plan for where I was going.

I couldn't let the stress go until I arrived in Annapolis, Maryland, and visited my sister Patty and her family. She took time off from work so we could be together.

We went to Washington, D.C., and checked out the sights. She also bought some Maryland crabs and we had a family crab boil. What a great time being with family!

I remember going with her to the Amish furniture and gift factory and with her husband Mike to the Space and Aeronautical museum. Finally, I had no stress and could get on with my trip of a lifetime.

If you take a vacation, go for at least three weeks! That's my advice. You really can't unwind with a week-long trip especially if you're traveling a long distance.

My sister complemented me on my trailer and kept saying, "This is really cool!" It made me feel great! Anytime you can sincerely compliment a person, don't hesitate to do it! That person will love you more and more.

Family heals your heart and gives you all kinds of advice. It is very important to stay close and be very open when communicating with them. Blood is thick!

Chapter 8
Sports and Exercise

******

No, that doesn't mean going to the bar and watching football on Sunday! It means working out, getting into shape and become a super-fighting machine. Diet and exercise go hand in hand.

Going to the bar with my friend Jimbo and watching football at the Purple Porpoise in Satellite Beach, Florida, was a fantastic time. We really enjoyed each other's company.

It absolutely did nothing for my health and wellness, but it helped me learn about becoming competitive. Watching football on Sunday and yelling at the TV for the players to run faster before being tackled was really fun.

One thing that was fun was meeting new friends, and to my surprise, making CONTACTS. Contacts watch and bet on sports. They can assist you sometimes in unexpected ways!

I miss Jimbo and his wife Trish. Jimbo passed away recently and he is sorely missed. I really miss his humor. I fell out of a bar chair once--not because I was drunk--but because he made me laugh so hard. If you are stressed, try to laugh! It isn't easy, but it is very soothing. People with great motivation can make other people forget their problems with humor. Why not try to take life a little easier and LAUGH once in a while.

Working out and getting your heartbeat up for a short time can make you forget about problems. I have found it actually helps you solve problems. It gets you out of the same old mode.

Hard physical activity is the best way to get in shape. When I say hard physical activity, I mean running wind sprints, heavy weight lifting and doing pull-ups and push-ups. Three things happen when you work out hard. You forget about the stress you're under, you get in shape and you look and feel great! It must be ROUTINE and completed every day for about 30 minutes. Exercising every day at the same time becomes habit and is recommended. In my opinion, a hard workout produces the best results.

That doesn't necessarily mean playing tennis or ping-pong. Although I really like these exercises, I feel the harder you work out, the better you become.

When I was in the Air Force, we had to do a physical exercise test every year. My age group had to complete a mile and a half in 14 minutes and 30 seconds or less. It wasn't too hard to complete if you trained throughout the year. It worked if you had an exercise ROUTINE.

Nearly everybody I knew was running before the test for about two weeks. I was one of those people. It killed me every year! Why? I was out of shape, had no motivation to be in shape and didn't follow a ROUTINE to STAY IN SHAPE!

I also like playing full-court basketball, softball, swimming and baseball. Not only do you meet a lot of nice people, you meet CONTACTS. You may say, "I hate to work out." Well, most people do! You're not alone!

Become motivated right now and DO IT. If you're busy at work, just take a walk after work and smell the roses. Working out completely reprograms your mind if you work out hard. It cleanses all your worries. Joining a gym is O.K. as long as you do something when you get there! A lot of times you go to the sauna and avoid working out. I bet you have! Don't fall in this trap.

I tried to stay in shape on my "Journey". I always tried to find campsites that were private. I loved going to campgrounds with a lot of space in between rigs. Sometimes I would take long walks and hike up on mountain ridges. I bought a nice camera before I left and was always taking pictures, loading them on the computer and emailing them to family and friends.

Sometimes, I would jog and other times I would chop firewood. I tried fishing or repairing the trailer as needed. There was always something to do.

It was really fun. One day I gave up coffee. That was tough! I lasted about a month and went back. I found I was too hyper at times. I usually got up early and was in bed before 9 p.m. I know, it sounds boring, but it worked for me.

If you work out, your heartbeat is elevated, you've broken a sweat and you're out of breath. Stretch out your muscles. Many injuries are caused by not stretching before and after exercise. Don't eat or exercise after 8 p.m.. Let your mind and stomach rest. Stop putting food in your mouth.

Sometimes I have eaten very late. It's OK to do it sometimes, just not every night. Sometimes if you eat the wrong foods, you will pay dearly. If I eat Italian food before bed, I pay for it. Thank goodness for antacids!

FOCUS, FOCUS, FOCUS when you work out! Don't fall into the trap of making the gym a social club. Focus on your workout and do so with DETERMINATION! The art of people-watching is another diversion. Exercise is necessary and will produce results if you stick with it. Work out and get out of your house.

When is the last time you took a walk? Was it three weeks or three months ago? I was never much of a walker until one day around Christmastime. I walked downtown in a historic part of Melbourne before the annual Christmas parade. Not too many people were out, but examining the 100+ year-old buildings and doing some window-shopping was fun. Some of the shops were very creative; some were firetraps like the used bookstore. The short walk was so much fun that it motivated me to walk the next day, and I made it a habit each day.

Opening your sniffer is a good way to clear your mind. Some cultures use smudging with sage or incense burning to clear the evil spirits in the house. I personally like the smell of incense or sage burning. They are also very relaxing to watch burn. If you have a smoke detector, turn it off during this exercise. You don't want the fire department responding!

I also am a big fan of water flowing. Waterfalls are my favorite. The arduous hike to the falls not only helps you observe beautiful things but it is also very soothing. Have you ever listened and focused on a waterfall for 10 minutes?

If you do, you will be caught up in the moment and not want to leave! This is especially true if you see the power of Niagara Falls. I call it Viagra Falls for the honeymooners. I totally was in awe when I saw a million gallons of water per minute fall off the cliff. If you haven't seen it, get on the first flight out! I was amazed and stayed the entire day just watching the force of water.

Have you ever noticed the water sounds in a day spa? Aren't they soothing? This is another place you don't want to leave. STRESS relief is extremely important for your body's recharge ability. Sometimes you have to watch the clock to make sure you don't stay all day. I guess that's why they call it a day spa!

Sometimes, I like to just sit and veg in front of the TV. I also like to go to the movies. You must limit this activity. If you don't, you won't be motivated to move. MOVEMENT IS MOTIVATION!

If you don't do something motivating, everything stays the same. I have probably spent a year of my life watching TV. That's way too much! Get out of the chair and turn it off. Limiting noise in your life will also decrease stress. Turn down the radios and TVs.

My wife and I were feeling unmotivated one day and decided to join a gym. We got a "special" off the Internet at 24-Hour Fitness. We got on our workout clothes and drove over to work out.

When we arrived at the Waikiki Club, we received a "free" personal trainer session with a man named Kendu. He was a very soft-spoken gentleman with absolutely no fat who was in fantastic shape. He taught us both how to do squats and exercise the "core" muscles.

I don't know about you but my core muscles aren't in shape! I was sore for two days after Kendu got done with me! You can always find out how out of shape you're in when you start an exercise program.

After we were taught stretching exercises, Kendu quietly mentioned they had a "special" for $99 to get three sessions with him. He said, "I have a few more exercises to show you." He teased us with a little and we bought a lot!

The next Saturday Kendu added more moves to the exercises. I could hardly walk out of the gym. He was such a soft sell, soft-spoken guy, you didn't realize you were exercising until you walked out of the gym and climbed some stairs.

Kendu used questions like, "How do you feel?" and "Did you eat before you came?" He really motivated us to eat several meals during the day and work out during the work out session!

Movement and positive words cause motivation. If you or somebody you respect says something positive, your outcome will always be better. Use and listen to motivating WORDS!

Exercise is important, as they say. It only causes pain when you're doing it and for two days after you're done!

Be careful and ask your doctor before you do any kind of physical program.

Purchasing the right clothes or uniforms is very important. Proper workout clothes, shoes, helmets, and goggles make your workout safer and more enjoyable.

If your mind sits, your body sits. If mind moves, your body moves. If you have passion, joy and peace, motivation will follow. Remember, negative energy is heavier than positive energy. The whole process of motivation requires you to change your bad habits into good ones.

I am sitting and thinking of good thoughts. Use your mind for good thoughts, not bad.

Challenge yourself to do some sort of exercise every day. It only takes a few minutes, and you will feel great. My psychology teacher at Northern Arizona University told us to do exercise for at least one month. If you try anything for at least a month, you will keep the habit.

Repeat after me, "I am going to exercise everyday for 30 minutes the rest of my life"! Say that 10 times to yourself today and two times the rest of your life. Now go and DO IT!

Working out isn't hard. It just takes motivation to get going. This is another reason to get outside and do something physical like aerobics, tennis or walking.

Thank you again for buying this book. It probably has helped you take your worries to another place. Nothing's better than reading a book to move your mind in fantasyland. When you are quiet, visualize where you want to go, as the famous Olympic coach said.

Chapter 9

Self-Sabotage

******

What a concept! There are many definitions for this concept. I believe self-sabotage is either your conscious or subconscious mind blocking you from succeeding in a task.

Sometimes during our upbringing, we are fine-tuned by our parents to get all "As" at school. Some parents value education so much that they say, "If Billy did it, you can do it."

Sometimes this pressure damages our confidence levels. Everyone has different styles and if you try to please everyone, your individuality will become lost. Do your best in everything.

Sometimes I have impeded my own success by waiting until the last minute to prepare. PROCRASTINATING is SELF-SABOTAGE! It also creates a whole bunch of unneeded stress in your life.

Another way to undermine your effectiveness is to not be a risk taker. We also sometimes speak softly not to be heard or do just enough to get by. I had that habit. My wife

Rebecca would always say "What?" She told me I mumbled. I worked very hard to change. I try now not to be lazy and speak clearly.

When you travel with a trailer, steps have to be taken to prepare for departure. You have to back your vehicle up and lower the trailer on the ball, roll up the wheel on the yoke, and attach the safety chains, power cord and sway bar. You have to roll up the awning, lift the steps back in place, unhook the power and water hose and detach the sewer line. I am certain there is more, but I can't remember at this point.

You have to put everything away inside and remove the TV from the stand and place it on the bed. You have to remember to make sure the refrigerator is closed and the shampoo is put away. You must remember to make sure the dirty dishes are put in the sink and roll down the TV antenna. Don't forget to close the roof vent. I am certain there is more, but I can't remember at this point.

When you pull out of the parking spot, it is always good to get out and recheck to make sure everything is tied down and put away. I am certain there is more, but I can't remember at this point.

Do you see how I sabotaged myself? Do you think it would have been wise to write all these steps down? You probably know what's going to happen now. I forgot one of the steps.

As I was leaving one day in Maine, I forgot to crank up the little wheel that holds the front of the trailer. It allows you to unhook the trailer from the vehicle. I drove away and heard a scraping noise. I got out and the wheel shaft was bent pretty badly. I got my trusty hammer out after saying a few choice words and pounded it back in place.

Once I forgot to close the refrigerator. When I arrived at my destination, I had a huge mess with ketchup and the previous night's beef stew all over the carpet. What a dummy I am!

Another incident happened when I scratched the side of my trailer with branches. I simply got too close to a tree. I scratched the paint a little bit. It wasn't too bad. I didn't have to cuss too much!

One day there was an older man hooking up his rig to leave. I started up a conversation with him. He didn't say a word until he was done. I was a little beside myself but waited for him to respond to all my questions.

I learned a valuable lesson from him when he said, "I don't talk to anybody when I am hooking up my RV". He said, "If I did, I would forget something very important. I am in a zone when I pack up to leave."

These words have stuck with me to this day. Always have a CHECKLIST when you are doing multiple tasks. I guarantee you will forget something. It may cause you or

in each person on your team and have one common goal to win.

Are you doing the task in the quickest, most accurate manner? You can get it done faster if you have the proper tools. Always learn something new. Your mind will thank you for it. Take charge and get motivated. Love it and do it.

Always keep your fan base and home team happy. Your significant other will respect you if you are a winner and will strive to help you win. If you are a loser, your partner will de-motivate their feelings for you and lose respect. Respect is earned.

There comes a time when you tried everything possible, you are satisfied with your effort and it just doesn't work. You become depressed, discouraged and unmotivated. It's time to quit, move on and get some help.

If you've done everything possible to complete the task and you really honestly gave it your all, don't beat yourself up; SEEK HELP. Sometimes changing professions or turning the project over to a co-worker with more experience can change the outcome. Sometimes, it isn't you. It's the impossible.

I recall a time when I was going to replace my hot water heater in the house. (I still don't understand why they call it hot water heater. It really is a cold water heater because that's what it does!) Anyway, I decided I was going to do it myself and not call a plumber.

I looked at the fittings, pipe, and tools needed to do the job. I checked on pricing for the hot water heater and it was about $250. I was just about to buy the unit and then I decided to get a price from a plumber. He wanted $350 installed. He would even haul the old one away for that price. I hired him to be there at 9 a.m. on Saturday.

As I watched him change out the unit, I noticed he used a torch, solder, a pipe wrench, fittings and a whole bunch of other tools I didn't have! In fact, it would have cost me more to buy the tools and change it myself! He was out in 45 minutes! I had the rest of the day to myself.

Sometimes, you need to ASK and PAY for a professional's help. By doing this, you will save hours of time (in my case, a whole lot of scraped knuckles). Remember to "eat crow" sometimes and ask for help.

Respect is hard to achieve, but you can do it by becoming the strongest match in the matchbox. You don't want to be the dullest knife in the block. Study all the time and learn something new each and every day.

******

Chapter 10
Humor

Milton Berle said, "Laughter is an instant vacation." If you don't have humor, you don't have any fun! Stress happens all the time. Medical bills, household bills, food bills, and family situations cause stress. Having a nasty divorce or a bad relationship can cause even more of the "S" word. Humor or "ha,ha,ha" relieves the pain. I hope you laughed!

Sometimes nothing seems to go right in life. The only way to cure this problem is to laugh it off. Laughter is inner jogging, according to Norman Cousins.

I remember when my good friend Digger was in Oahu for heart surgery. His wife was all alone when I arrived to visit him after the surgery. I remember her sadness when I arrived, but her positive attitude was shining. I started to crack jokes while we waited for him to get out of surgery. I'll admit when he was late coming back to the room, I was pretty worried. She was in better spirits by the time he came out.

Finally, Digger arrived smiling. I blew up a rubber glove and drew a picture on the glove so they would remember my visit and not the hurt they had just gone through. I also left his favorite golf magazine and chocolate for her. They never · forgot it.

Here are some exercises you can use to relieve stress:

1. You must stop and BREATHE. Not short breaths but deep meditation breaths. Do this for eight seconds. Most people go seven seconds, but you are a champion and will hang in for eight seconds, won't you?

2. Look at the problem with an open mind. Ask internal questions of your self, like "Are my loved ones in danger? Is it necessary that I leave right now, or can I attend to it tomorrow? Can you simply walk away from the problem at hand?

3. Ask yourself how you can make this a winning situation. Compartmentalize your feelings. There are times to break down and times to be tough. Always allow yourself to have release but do so when it benefits you.

4. Refocus through gratitude and prayer. Be thankful for what you have and pray for what you don't (within reason).

5. Teasing is a release. Before you go out and tease somebody, let me tell you my wife hates it. So be careful whom you tease.

6. Everybody is motivated--even crooks! Crooks are motivated before they rob the bank, and animals are

motivated to find food for survival. Motivation has to be pumped up. Get past your past and move on.

Have you ever laughed so hard it hurt? That is a great feeling. You totally forget about your problems. Do you have a family member or friend who makes you laugh? Go visit them!

I love going to comedy clubs. The crowd is waiting to get inside and simply laugh. The crowd is buzzing. People are saying, "I heard Bobby is really funny." You are pumped up because you know you're going to laugh. What a great feeling to have!

Laughter cures problems! Laugh it off! My boss Don is a jokester. All day he cracks jokes. Most aren't very good, but effort counts!

For Don's birthday, we got him a children's joke book. He told us jokes all day from the book. After we stopped laughing, he decided to give it to his five-year-old granddaughter. I am sure she told jokes and punished her parents for weeks with that book!

Comedy shows, funny movies and clowns at the circus make us laugh. Some doctors say laughing keeps your blood pressure down, and you live longer. Well, then try laughing! It works!

Chapter 11

Romance in Motivation

******

I read several books about how to become romantic after divorce or a breakup. They were BEST SELLERS that I recommend you read and keep in your library. They will keep you informed of the current events in the changing world. Hopefully, you won't be in these situations!

These books taught me a few things about finding the right woman and how to take care of her. It was kind of a motivation for the romantic guy type book. Although on occasion I still need help in this department; the motivation is still there and I continue to try.

That reminds me of the saying, "You can't always get what you want." This is especially true if you try too hard or are not telling the truth. People pick up on "being pushy".

You must be ON when you want something. You must also prioritize your life (GOALS) on what your motivation of being ON is going to be. In other words, "What do you want and how can you get it?"

Sometimes when we're "in the moment," romance is the greatest motivation we can feel. It's like the first date. You take a shower, shave and clean up, worry about what you are going to say and PLAN the evening. You look sharp and try your best to arrive ON-TIME.

You drive up hoping you make a great first impression. Maybe you planned ahead and took a dry run the day before in order to find where the date lives. Maybe you even put on some good-smelling stuff and moussed your hair! As you walk out to the car, are you fumbling the keys? You are very nervous.

You're ready for the door to open. You have your dinner reservations confirmed, you washed your car, and now you drive up and knock on the door. DEEP BREATH!

Did you buy something for your date like flowers or candy? Did you bring your PROPOSAL? Do you understand what's happening? You are planning a sales presentation in a certain kind of way. You're getting ready to sell yourself!

Are you seeing how planning is extremely important? If you didn't plan, you won't get a second date or any kind of buying signals! Buying signals, or "I hope they like me," are extremely important in your motivation. Without them, you will not close the sale, deal or proposal.

As you walk to the car door, do you open the door? Do you open the door at the restaurant? Did you have all your tools in place to accomplish the goal? This may sound very mechanical, but that's what motivation is.

Romance and motivation go hand in hand. If you weren't motivated to go on the date, you wouldn't have asked the person out! If you weren't motivated, you wouldn't have PLANNED.

The goal may be getting a goodnight kiss or a chance at another date. If you aren't closing during the date or "business" meeting, chances are you won't get return business! Am I right? You bet I am!

So after dinner, you open the door, get in the car and go to a movie. Did you confirm which movie is good? Did you find a paper with reviews before you left the house? Did you have all the tools in place to make a great impression?

Romance and motivation go together. If you weren't motivated, you wouldn't have asked the person out! NO MOTIVATION EQUALS NO PLANNING, AND NO RESULTS WILL FOLLOW.

The buying sign or motivation is an agreement between two people. If you don't feel a connection or motivation toward each other, there won't be a second date. I hope this wasn't too uneasy or disconcerting for you, but a great motivational moment requires PLANNING and EXECUTION.

As I was reminded, all this looks like a business plan. Where's all the romance? Aren't you romantic? I am! When you are out on that date, treat your mate with respect, open the doors and have fun. You will have much more fun if you do. Believe it!

Manners go a long way when it comes to getting along with people. They work for both men and women. Nobody likes somebody negative, boring or just plain stupid! Hopefully, before you asked them out you would know this. Did you pre-qualify?

But sometimes you won't know the qualities about a person for years. Even if you get married, you may find faults with your mate many years later. It isn't something you can't handle. It means becoming positive will help you overcome your differences.

Most likely, you will hear the words, "You weren't like that before we were married." Well, you can overcome these bad traits with motivation. Motivate yourself to IMPROVE. You should be on a continuous cycle for lifelong improvement. Always always seek self-improvement!

Hopefully, you will find a mate who calls you on your faults! It usually is very motivating when you hear it in stereo and at high volume!

Always, always, continue to improve your body, mind and spirit. You must strive to be the best in order to become the best. That's an old saying, but still holds true today.

Chapter 12

Rest

******

I go to bed early. I am an early riser and not a night person. You may be one or the other. Use what works for you to create the most positive and motivating outcome. People are different. They decide if they need sleep or stay up late.

You and only you determine when you have had enough and decide to sleep. The goal of resting is to wake up optimized and refreshed. Say the word sleep to yourself right now. Say, "I want to sleep." Saying it relaxes you. The words "rest" and "sleep" are recharging when done. Taking naps are really nice on Sunday afternoons watching golf on TV.

I went to the beach one day and was enjoying the sun and relaxation. The beach was great, especially when I cooled off in the water. I looked around and watched the other people enjoy the fun with their families.

Suddenly, I noticed three people texting with their cell phones. Wow, give it a break for a few hours! Smell the fresh salt air and enjoy the sun. Relaxing means take it easy and refresh the body, mind and spirit.

In the military you were issued leave or vacation. You could accumulate a certain amount and if you didn't use it, you lost it. The government wanted you to take some time off to recharge. One day, this guy came back from leave. He'd had to use 30 days or lose it. I talked to him and asked what he did? He said, "Nothing." I said, "Didn't you go on vacation or leave town?" He said he didn't have any money, and his family stayed home.

The reason we take time off is to relax. Isn't that right? Save your money and take a nice vacation. Visit family and friends or see a historic site. Don't just stay home and fix the house or wash your windows. Get on a plane, train or automobile and leave town.

Why do we spend more time preparing for a vacation than our job? Why don't we write down what we're supposed to accomplish the next day at work? You probably know the answer. Work isn't important to us. Work is work and not a motivator for us. Vacations and resting are better!

When we go on a trip, we plan. We buy the airline tickets; get the best deal on hotels and rent-a-cars. We work at packing, buy new clothes, get some sporting goods and enjoy the adventure in our mind. We can't wait to get on the plane and go. We even have a checklist written on what to pack and take with us.

I have back problems every so often. I try to do exercises to make my back stronger, but on occasion, I get tremendous pain from sitting wrong. It's a way for my body to tell me to take time off and rest. Stress and picking up things incorrectly can cause you to suffer back pain. Relax, use your legs when lifting and see a doctor if the pain doesn't get better!

Why aren't we organized at work that makes us money? Why don't we plan for the next day, week, or year at our job? Maybe we're lazy, it's not important or we think it's just a J-O-B. It is your family's livelihood. Work hard and then play hard. Not in reverse.

It is very important to take it easy. Sometimes you need a real break. I mean do absolutely really get away. Just sit, try to catch a fish and look at the water. Most people can't do it. They simply have to be doing something all the time. Why do you suppose people have stress? Watch yourself and your health. Spend quality time with you.

Chapter 13
Water

******

Have you ever noticed how calm you get when you hear running water? Some of the best decisions I've made were in the shower! Water is a powerful energy and is called the universal solvent.

Water cleanses, refreshes, helps plants and wildlife grow and is necessary for life to exist. Why do you suppose water is so calming? Why do you think you need to drink eight glasses of water a day? I bet you aren't measuring how much you really do drink. I bet you drink less water than you really need. Drink up!

You have to STOP and LISTEN to the water flow over rocks, in streams and on the sand. Stop and listen to water's power and movement. You will become refreshed, centered, and motivated once again.

I like hiking to waterfalls. Strenuous hiking and exercise cleans the mind and helps you get back in shape. It also breaks the routine. Remember, if your creative mind isn't refreshed, it becomes stale. If you are doing the same thing each day like watching four hours of TV, it becomes ROUTINE. If you get in the same routine, you will lose creativity and grow old!

I suggest you incorporate water in your environment. It doesn't have to be expensive like installing a $40,000 swimming pool or an expensive water fountain, but maybe a small table sized fountain. You could design your room around the water like a Zen house with cool colors, or buy a lake or oceanfront home.

Fishing is relaxing! You also get recharged and develop a skill like casting the line or baiting the hook. What's really fun is catching a fish without going to the local grocery store. Deep-sea fishing is really fun especially if somebody else owns the boat and pays for the gas. The Sun is involved in this process. I would say 90 percent of the time when you travel on a boat, you will become refreshed. This isn't true if you become sea sick!

Swimming is a good exercise. You become tired (a goal), and develop your breathing. You definitely develop your arms and legs and feel great when you're done. In Honolulu, Waikiki beach is a famous attraction. I walked sometimes through the hotels to enjoy the waterfalls. Water attractions in hotels are relaxing if you stay in a "quiet zone" away from distractions. I just love the sound of water and the beauty of all the foliage.

Sometimes on the info commercials, you see people "getting rich" in front of a pool for the "get rich" schemes. Occasionally, there are some people who do make money on these programs. But usually, they are few and far between.

The get rich schemes usually don't work. HARD WORK, WORKS! Hard networking, hard work and the desire to win, makes dreams come true.

Go to NIAGARA FALLS! Plan on it, see it and make it happen. Say to yourself, I will see Niagara Falls. You won't believe your eyes when you see one million gallons of water per second fall down. What an amazing amount of power!

Water is good mixed in green tea which I recommend you drink. I don't want to get into health and nutrition in this book, but you know it's important to DIET. It isn't fun, but is necessary. I admit I have trouble when I travel keeping the weight off with all the good food out there.

If you are a coach and win the football game, you may get drenched with a cooler full of Gatorade if you win the big game. Not that's got to be refreshing.

One day it was raining very hard in Waikiki. My wife and I decided to go to the other side of Oahu to the North Shore. As we drove on the Liki Liki highway to Kanohe, the rain let up and it ended, becoming a perfect day. If we hadn't challenged the weather and left the house, we never would have experienced such a nice day.

Rain is important for growth. If it rains, we shouldn't be upset we should thank God for giving us new life. I hope you understand and experience the power of water. You really need to see it, touch it, and feel the greatness it provides. It is an amazing energy.

Chapter 14
Safety Sticker

※※※※※※

There once was a man who needed a safety sticker. He used his motivation to overcome the problem and succeeded in his goal.

In some states, you are required to obtain a state inspection safety sticker for your car: going to a mechanic and having your car checked to see if the turn signals, brake light, and headlights are working. The sticker was due by the end of January for this man, so he set out to find a mechanic on the last day of the month, which happened to be on a Saturday.

The man had an older car that had been channeled or lowered over the frame to be closer to the ground. You probably can figure what's going to happen now. So he set out on his "journey" finding what should be a simple operation that costs about $15 dollars.

It was Saturday, and everybody who had a sticker due in January was doing the same thing, and mechanics closed by 12 noon. He pulled in to the first shop, and the first thing the man did was tell him he needed to remove all the window tinting as it was too dark. The man told him it was on the car when he bought it from the dealer. The mechanic told him, "How do I know that?"

As the man drove to the next service station, he was wondering if he really did need to remove this safety film. He went to his regular mechanic who was having trouble renewing his license through the state. The state was creating tougher standards for mechanics and making them take tests to renew their licenses. After the man got his car washed he moved on to the next location.

At the third stop, the man was told he has to remove the metal holder under the license plate that held the safety sticker for years. The man said it was on the car, approved by the dealer when he bought it and the dealer accomplished the safety paperwork. Nothing doing, so he went to mechanic number 4.

This mechanic told him he needed to remove the lowered plastic mud flap and could do it for $200. By now, the man was figuring out the entire safety process. It was built so auto repair could make money. Since this man didn't have any extra money to spend, he was off to mechanic numbers 5 and then to 6.

Number 5 told him he would have to pay $70 to the state to inspect to see whether the car had been lowered properly and before that, needed to have an $80 front-end alignment which he could do in about two hours' time. Mechanic number 6 was inspecting the car and stopped at the window that didn't go up and down. He said the motor was broken, need to be replaced, and could do it for $275

The man was feeling his heart beat hard; his left arm was hurting and he found himself cussing at the top of his lungs with the window closed; that didn't work. He realized everybody needs to support their family and knew in his heart that it was for safety, but he could only spend $15 today or face a ticket of $75 if he drove the car.

As his heart was racing, his screaming was diminishing and he came to his senses, the man said, "I am going to get this done today?". He said, "Nothing is going to stop me and I want a safety sticker now!" Right after he said it, he saw an old man at another gas station doing safety checks. He pulled right in, made the mechanic laugh, heard his complaining about everybody waiting till the last minute, and paid $15 for a safety check. The old man didn't question anything on his car, did the simple check, and got the job done in 12 minutes and 30 seconds. SUCCESS!

Have you learned something about never giving up? Did you learn it takes more than five "No's to get a "Yes" in sales? Did you learn if you put out the energy, think about the problem and never, ever give up, chances are you will succeed in your goal? That man did. Thank goodness his wife wasn't with him in the car. He would never have heard the end of it!

it, and then I thought about the years and years of prayers and sadness that structure experienced. So many people had come in and out and prayed inside that church for centuries. There has to be something out there, so always keep your faith and pray.

When I was traveling in the RV I focused on feeling the turns and the road up ahead. A few times, I didn't look at the map. I just let the road take me where it wanted to go. It was the most out of body experience I ever felt. Some days, I was very lonely and decided to pray while I was driving. It always made me feel better. To this day, I still pray. So PRAY! It really takes your mind off the problems and motivates you to do the right thing.

Sometimes, I would feel where to turn in my arms. I know, it sounds crazy, but it really happened. I remember one Sunday when I was traveling through Indiana and looking for a church to attend. It was about 9 a.m. and used my mind to lead me to a church. I know, it sounds crazy, but that was about the fourth month on the road and I was really in tune to my body. Most days, I didn't know what day it was! I was traveling on a long freeway and suddenly told myself I got to stop and go to church! I pulled off the next exit and went to the gas station. The gas station was very isolated. I filled up the tank and started driving. As I pulled onto the road, something told me to turn right and not left. It was very strange, but I went with it.

As I traveled, I noticed a little town and a cross on top of a steeple. I pulled the RV into the parking lot and went to church. It was a very strange feeling, but I was pulled off the freeway to that church. Have you ever been led to a positive outcome? Always take the chance.

It was like I was led by a very powerful energy. Sometimes you have to go with what leads you and discard the rest or "go with the flow". You will become your own motivator if you follow the right path.

As I reflect on this chapter, I remember the amazing things that have happened in my life when I kept the faith. I think REFLECTING is very important in clearing your mind and calming yourself. Sit quietly and talk to yourself if you want! It might be advisable to make sure nobody hears you.

Instead of talking with yourself, why don't you have a pad of paper with you and write your thoughts down. Remember all the notes you took during school lectures? Go back to those good old days and start writing down what's really on your mind.

Write 10 THINGS you like that are happening in your life right now. Instead of writing 10 things you don't like and becoming negative, write 10 things you do like. It is much more refreshing and enlightening. Write 10 THINGS YOU

WANT and 10 THINGS YOU NEED. Read them every single day twice a day until they all are completed.

As far as going to church, lately I have been trying to arrive early. Getting to church early without rushing is your chance to REFLECT/RECHARGE/RENEW. I sit in the car with all the noise off in TOTAL QUIET. By doing this, I become aware and my mind is open for the service. In church, listening to the message and focusing on the words, ring in your motivation, and your self-esteem. It brings you the power for the following week to be a WINNER.

Prayer also helps you become calm and slows your heartbeat. You will find it clears your mind, gives you solutions to problems and totally motivates you. Prayer will help you if you allow it in your daily life.

Chapter 18
Observation

******

Have you ever observed what other leaders do? Have you noticed their actions, words, demeanor, and positive attitude? I strongly recommend you notice today. OBSERVING revealed some of the most profound moments in my life.

Why do you suppose some people are leaders and some are followers? Do you think it is because they are better than others or were born with a silver spoon? Do you think they were just "lucky?" Chances are if you ASK THEM, you might find out how they became what they are. You may be very surprised by what they say.

Most people don't NETWORK. If you join a club that contains prominent leaders, do you think some of their success may rub off on you? You bet it will! Observation of who, what and where they are and how they do what they do is absolutely a huge key to success. Motivate yourself to surround yourself with leaders and observe what they are doing different. Some of the best leads I have received are from people on elevators. You're laughing now aren't you!

If you work in a high-rise building and are going up an elevator, ask questions like, "What floor are you on?" or "What do you do?" You have 20 seconds to find out. Chances are you will instantly have a contact that you will see again and again. Make sure you have your card to give them and ask for their card before you get off.

Immediately when you make a contact email the person a greeting like "It was very nice meeting you" and if you're really interested invite them to lunch. Motivate yourself to ask them calmly how they became successful and simply ask them, "Can you teach me how?" People generally like helping other people.

Right now I am sitting in a hotel lobby observing people and trying to make contact with business people. Usually in a high-end hotel or a business hotel you can make three contacts in two days without really working hard at it. The obstacle is you have to get out of your room and ask questions. At a business hotel people are usually resting at the bar or restaurant after a hard day's work. Always remember to ask for a business card and carry a pen with you.

You never know whom you are going to meet. Sometimes by sitting in a chair close to an elevator lobby with your laptop, people will come up to you and ask what you"re typing. People are generally curious about what others are doing. If you listen and watch them closely, you will find whom you need to approach.

I closely watch other motivational speakers to perfect my craft. I love to get motivated by sitting through a motivational speaker's presentation. I strongly recommend you watch others in action.

Chapter 19
Fishing and Relaxation

******

Relax and enjoy your day. Go fishing! Who cares if you catch anything? Who cares if you get sunburned? Who cares if you lose your bait? Get your hands dirty. It's fishing; it's the luck of the day, and if you keep hold of your tongue the right way (in your mouth), the benefits will outweigh the negatives.

Don't forget the fish stories you get to tell when you get home. I had a "big" one over two feet long and it broke the line! Wow, it was really cold and the fish weren't biting!

You always become a different person when you go outdoors. The vitamin D is great! In my life, some of the greatest experiences have been on a boat. I have always felt the best when I am doing nothing but trying to catch a fish. Who cares if you catch the big one? You're OUTDOORS and are experiencing a fantastic experience called NATURE.

While we are on the subject, have you turned off the TV today? I bet you are reading this book with the TV on.

Remember to limit noise from your life. Fishing usually keeps you away from the noise of city life.

As I'm writing this chapter, I am sitting by the pool soaking in rays. I have my sunscreen on, and the weather is perfect. Doctors recommend sunscreen; therefore, make sure you have it on. Pay attention to the professionals.

Let's talk a minute about swimming, tennis, running, or whatever sport you like to do. Just get out and do it. Have you ever noticed how pumped up an athlete is? They are high-strung, self motivated to win and look and feel great. They may even live longer because they are in shape. The true athlete doesn't quit, doesn't like to lose, and never accepts the word can't. They don't stop, and they love to work out. They live it, talk about it and breathe it.

Why do they do it? They love to WIN. They love the challenge to push their body and mind to the limit. The thrill of victory excites them, competition runs in their blood. They simply love what they do and love to be OUTSIDE. They are truly motivated. Life isn't easy; life isn't fun, but winners always get it done.

Chapter 20

Looks

******

Good-looking people are all around us. They walk and talk with confidence. The clothes they wear allude to confidence and power/ Most of the time I like to dress down. For the longest time and still to this day, I love to wear shorts and hate wearing pants. Living in Hawaii allows me to wear shorts year round with temperatures in the 80s most of the time.

Sometimes wearing shorts or dressing down eliminates advancement in promotions, meeting quality contacts, and business leads. You see, people notice what you wear and especially what's on your feet. Shoes sometimes dictate success. Most people when they walk look down and will notice your shoes before they notice you.

Beautiful people get me motivated to look my best. In Hawaii, it is very rare to see someone in a suit. It is very easy to become lax and not wear my best. I challenge you to shop for nice clothes and always look your best. It will be motivating to you to primp in the mirror; look at yourself closely and notice you really may need to lose a couple of pounds to become motivated again.

Sometimes, it works to your advantage to dress down. I usually dress down when I buy or get my car repaired at a mechanic. I want to give the impression that I don't have any money. If I look sloppy, I usually get a better price because they feel sorry for me! Isn't that great! You bet it is and your checking account thanks you.

You hear a lot about entrepreneurs who wear blue jeans to board meetings, shorts to sales calls and drive raggedy old cars. They want to fit in and leave a comfortable impression to their clients. Sometimes this works against them and they don't get the sale. I have always found you never go wrong dressing up for a sales call unless you are going to an industrial area. Sometimes the profession you are in dictates what you wear.

One thing everybody can do is practice good hygiene! Take a shower and comb your hair. Be clean! You attract what you wear! Do you believe this? Try it today. Wear some really nice clothes; visit a high-end hotel, business establishment or an art gallery. You will be amazed at the end of the day what you have become. A connected, well rounded professional who is articulate and worldly. You will most likely have HUGE POCKETFUL OF LEADS at the end of the day. People will be attracted to you. Isn't that motivating?

As I walk down the hall, I am very aware what other people wear. I found myself becoming critical until my "ground control" or my wife called me on it. Ground control keeps you on track! I told her, "No, I am not critical" for more than three months, and then I realized I was. She was right and I was wrong. Ok, I said it and really hated to be the way I was. What do you think happened to me?

By thinking others were less than me and putting them down, I was attracting lower self-esteem for myself and attracted low results. I was never verbal to the other people, but thought about it. NEVER BE CRITICAL OF OTHERS! People are people and always will be people. Take your mind off them and don't judge. Just say "Good morning" and move on. I am especially kind to the elderly.

Don't be mad at anybody. Just let it go! Sometimes you really want to avoid negative people. You should avoid people when your safety is in jeopardy, but don't be rude. If you ask several questions, people will open up to you. All people have a story, and if you can make their day by making them laugh, you will feel like a million bucks. Tell jokes, be current on events of the day, and avoid negative comments. You will make a great friend.

As I am writing this at the pool, I am sitting next to a couple of ladies who look to be in their 70s. I am writing and can hear what they are saying by eavesdropping with one ear. They are wondering what I am doing. Curiosity is driving them crazy. They will soon ask me what I am doing. She asked me, "What are you writing?" I explained I was writing a book on motivation.

I asked, "Where are you from?" and "What did you do before you retired?" "Who is your favorite politician?" I got a lot of information with those questions and made another friend. She lived in Dallas, her husband died 20 years ago, she remarried, got a divorce and owns two houses. She liked Barry Goldwater, and her husband was an American Airlines pilot before he died.

You get the idea. EVERYBODY HAS A STORY! All you have to do is ask! They love talking about themselves. As I was talking to her, she told me her friend's husband, two chairs over, was an author of financial books. Wow, what a contact!

Curiosity killed the cat. So she asked me what I was doing, and said she liked what I was writing and was interested in my motivation to create a book. She was impressed with me, and I guarantee she will tell her friends she met an author. I am not tooting my own horn but want to demonstrate all you have to do is ASK QUESTIONS. People love to brag, boast and tell you what they do, who they know, and what they are going to do. It's their way of motivating themselves, telling you about them.

Asking the question, "What's the weather going to do today?" always brings a response. It is always a good icebreaker. The goal is to TALK to a stranger and find out what makes that person tick. You also can ask for advice after asking a few questions and getting to know them. You never know, they may know someone who can help you.

If people like you, they may also want to invest in your project. The old adage, "You got to know someone," is right on the money. How do you get to know someone? Well, you have to TALK!

If you're shy, talking is hard to do. Talking is simple if you ask, "What's happening?" People usually say something if you ask them this question. Remember, people love to talk about themselves and like to know what's going on in the world. Don't be shy. Just force yourself to talk. It will bring tremendous results.

Become a "MENTAL MOTIVATOR" in your life. Always think and ask yourself, "What can I do to make things better"? If you are already there, then REST and take a mind regeneration break. Being up all the time is tiring and can sap your energy. Take time to recharge.

I can tell you I am not motivated every minute of the day. Nobody is. When I am motivated, I become the best at my craft and work hard to complete as many tasks I can.

Chapter 21
Light-ups

✳✳✳✳✳✳

Have you ever seen people who light up a room? They absolutely bring out the best in people with their excitement and enthusiasm. They exude confidence and nothing gets them down. You always remember their name, want to talk to them and love their style.

They are winners! People love to talk with winners. You can do the same thing! It's what I call LIGHT-UPS! These people beam when they walk, smile when you meet them and build you up. Light-ups are magnets. They connect with everyone around them. You can do the same thing.

You know, these people may owe, owe, owe, but you don't know unless you ask pointed questions like "What do you do?" You must find out if you want to do business with them. They could drain your enthusiasm! Some are the best liars in the business, and some are for real. If they have shifty eyes, use caution.

You can become a light-up by walking, talking and creating positive energy around you. Light-ups usually remember your name. I am no expert at this, but you probably could go on line and punch up "how to remember names" and get some good advice.

It was getting hot and jumped into the pool. Afterwards the pool attendant told me not to dive. She really wanted to know what I was doing writing all day. I told her I was writing a motivation book. She asked me if I ever saw this other motivation book. I said yes I have, but mine is better. She loved my confidence. She read, "All you have to do is get out." She said this and I wondered if she was following what she said. Most people read it, get motivated for a day and then lose energy. So, after you read this book, keep that in mind: Never lose your energy; keep trying to be motivated.

You see, people always tell people what to do. We are trained to be the expert! But do we follow the rules? Do we really do what people and books say, or do we read and go back to our old ways. Are you going to read this book and go back to your old ways? I hope not! Follow these easy steps; get motivated to talk and be outside, and things will happen for you.

I said to her, "I would love to have a book signing here at the pool." She said that would be great! I thought to myself, you're right; it's going to be great. I plan on selling many books.

Chapter 22

Jobs

******

From experience I learned one important thing. You don't have the job until they offer it to you. So many people go to an interview, thinking it went well and end up not having the job. You must always continue searching for the job and continue your search until an employer offers you the money.

So many people quit after they interview thinking they have the job. NEVER QUIT. Continue "working" to find a job until you have it. You must work at finding a job as you would at a full time job.

Sadness, depression and relationship problems go hand in hand finding a job. Be aware of these problems, because they will come up. Count on it! Always strive to keep POSITIVE and never ever quit--never. You will eventually get what you are searching for and will be very proud of yourself.

JOB stands for Just Over Broke! Nobody loves their job; they just go because they have to survive. I have had several jobs, have hated some and liked several others. My dad kept the same job until he died. As I grew up in Casa Grande, my father worked very hard to support five kids who ate a great deal of food.

Many people try their best to keep the same job for 20 years and retire. Those days are gone! As economies get worse, the job market becomes more competitive. When unemployment goes up, you will find yourself looking harder to find a job and encountering more rejection. You must perform a simple life-changing action, and that is power up your GOOD ATTITUDE!

Always take time for family, exercise and alone time while looking for work. Finding a job is the toughest job on the planet. Treat it like a job working 8-5 everyday until you are employed.

Networking is important in your job search. Ask contacts this, "Do you know anybody who is hiring?" Never be too proud to ask that question. You will never know the answer unless you humble yourself now and again. You very well may be surprised what others say.

Owning a business (I don't want to work for somebody else) is a very lofty goal and I encourage it. The freedom to be your own boss is exciting! Remember one thing. You are the boss, and you will be challenged every day by putting in a lot of hours, nights and weekends.

Challenges will happen owning a business. I'll never forget the time when I owned my tanning salon in Palm Bay, Florida. I was out to a nice dinner on a Saturday night at Carraba's in Melbourne. Just after I finished eating a great steak, I got a call from one of my employees who said she didn't want to work anymore.

Boy was I angry! I got in my car, drove to the salon and sent her packing! I gave her a final paycheck, and took the keys to the cash register and the store. She was very surprised to see me! I had to take control of the situation and protect my livelihood. Success in business requires HARD WORK!

When I arrived in Honolulu from Maui, I worked my butt off trying to find a job. I went on 19 interviews in 31 days. I had to turn it around. You can imagine how my attitude changed after every rejection. I needed to pay bills and eat!

I had no luck finding a job using the Internet. I punished myself and cold-called businesses the old fashioned way. I asked if they had any openings. I had to be positive!

I must have filled out 50 applications printed and sent out 50 resumes.

The job pool was low and the number of applicants was high. What I am saying is NEVER QUIT, never give up and try, try, try. Interviewing is a tough business. You will go to several interviews in the job market.

I finally did find a job helping people find jobs. What an irony that was. I definitely had experience interviewing.

Sometimes it may take three to six months for an employer to hire you. You may have to interview five times before they give you the job. Remember, you don't have the job unless they offer it to you! Sometimes you will be called back five times. Don't get caught up waiting for a hiring authority to hire you. It may take three in-person interviews, and a meeting with higher management.

Are you positive? Are you really positive in your heart and mind? How can you continuously be positive? It takes EFFORT AND COMMITMENT never to say bad or think bad thoughts.

That's harder than it sounds. Sometimes you want to be negative because you're tired or irritable, have a migraine or somebody needs your mind. You're not going to be positive when this happens. You have to slow down and turn it around.

I personally found saying positive words to myself like WIN, helps me become positive. If you counteract negative words with positive ones, you will win, win and win again!

Reprogram that beam between your eyes. Make it a habit to think positive. Make your destiny become reality by saying positive words to yourself. Make a mental count of how many negative thoughts you say in one day. If you want to change, it takes two times more positive words than negative to change.

Try it right now. Keep going and don't quit. Say, "positive, positive, positive!" Rest and say "win, win, win." You get the picture! Don't you feel better? Reprogramming is absolutely vital to your success. If you want a negative outcome, think negative. It will come, I guarantee!

Chapter 23
Focus

******

Sometimes in life you need to slow and be observant. I have found this extremely helpful when I decided to write this book. It's called focus. Focus means a lot of things. Most people will yell at you to FOCUS! Some will tell you "You need to focus." Most will never explain what it means to focus.

I have found my wife very helpful in motivating me to keep focused. Sometimes she looks me right in the eye, uses heavy body language on me and tells me to focus. It totally freaks me out but calms me down so I will slow down and THINK.

My wife is a very important part of my life. Zig Zigler calls your family support "your home team." He tells us to always take care of the people you love. If you come home after a bad day, your "home- team" will provide you with the focus and determination you need to become motivated.

Sometimes I find focusing on an object like a flower or a blank space on a wall helps tremendously to solve problems in my mind. You may want to be careful. You will find that people may think you are kooky if you stare too long so that you may want to do this exercise only at home. Focusing on an object for a couple of minutes helps you cleanse your mind and gives you answers when you are struggling to accomplish the task.

"Focus" can mean anything. You can use your mind to read and memorize a speech or tell yourself you are going to make $10,000 dollars this month. You can motivate and focus on one thing and it will either happen or come very close to happening. The mind is powerful! Use it wisely.

Sometimes I focus and observe what energy is happening in a certain situation. If you go to a party for instance, you can tell immediately if the party will be dull or lively. It only takes one look at the participants and one scan of the room.

Everybody has heard if you focus on negativity, you will become negative. If you focus on POSITIVITY, you will become positive. This is a no-brainer, and I guarantee if you do this more than anything else, you will be more motivated, commanding, and a sure winner.

Great leaders have trouble sleeping because their minds don't stop or turn off. Some presidents worked on only four to five hours sleep.

If you remember from my previous chapters, I said, "When you sleep, you sleep." Usually, I fall asleep very quickly, but on occasion I have to focus on "nothing" to sleep. I found thinking about nothing really helps me sleep. I visualize an empty white space in my mind. Try it tonight if you can't sleep; it really works!

My current office overlooks buildings, and the ocean is in the background. Sometimes, I focus on the ocean or traffic driving by. People watching is always fun. If you spend a little time moving your mind from the present to how it used to be, you become a different person.

Chapter 24
Reading/Seminars/Tapes/ Computers

✳✳✳✳✳✳

To perfect yourself at motivation, you must constantly study, seek and listen to motivating speakers, read books and DO WHAT THEY SAY! We all get in the same old same old mode and need every so often a motivational TUNE-UP.

If you listen to speakers a couple of things will happen. One, you may learn new things, and two you may remember them. Once you understand what is said, you must keep up a MOTIVATION PLAN. Speakers who really motivate give you a feel good feeling that you can succeed, and they inspire you to become a better person.

Have you ever noticed the time that is wasted with gadgets? Sit on a bus and watch how many people are listening to music, playing with their cell phones, and calling someone! What is really fun is using your cell phone at an airport to brag you arrived in Atlanta. Some people say this to act important. Others have no life and can't communicate without something in their hands. Whatever happened to

Chapter 25
Rain, Snow, Sleet and Heat

******

Have you ever noticed when it rains people stay indoors? If it's hot outside, we stay home. If it's snowing or cold, people stay warm and don't dare go out in the cold! The exception to this rule is when you go to work, are on vacation or during an emergency. Sometimes people venture out to go to the movies, malls and museums during a good rainstorm.

The most important thing you can do is FORGET ABOUT IT and go outside. Raincoats, umbrellas, and rubber boots were invented to keep you dry. Use them and go outside!

Dealing with cold, sleet and snow isn't fun for traveling. Driving on wet roads, ice and snow isn't easy. If you don't want to drive, take a cab, bus or train.

What I am trying to convey is to go outside and see what happens to our environment when it's nourished by life-giving water. I am a firm believer that men and women are different when it comes to going outside. Women like to go on their terms and men could be there in a minute. Culture and dress dictate what is worn and who has to dress up before they are seen in public. I never have agreed with this, but it does help in business.

Traveling, doing something, seeing things grow, and watching things come alive is what nature is all about. You can't see this if you are locked indoors, lying on the couch watching TV.

You also will find that staying home sometimes brings out hostility in others. The atmospheric pressure and humidity rises. The lack of sun can make us depressed. Arrogance starts, closed in feelings begin and the lack of vitamin D is apparent.

Your motivation plan is to treat every day like it's sunny. The weather is perfect and sky is beautiful every day of your life. You absolutely love life every minute of the day. DO NOT COMPLAIN to others about the weather. If an outside influencer mentions how bad the weather is, turn it around to a positive statement. Say, "It will change soon; it always does." Memorize this powerful comeback.

Everything on the planet revolves around water, sunlight, and energy. Water has been called the "universal solvent." It totally cleanses the body. If you have a lack of any of these, you will become de-motivated. Tell your body right now, "Every day is perfect." (One more time) "Everything is Perfect."

Now the most important thing you can do is believe everything is perfect, everything will change for the better and everything is going to be all right. Say these things in your mind; repeat them every day and believe no matter how bad things seem; everything will become all right in the end. Needless worrying does nothing but cause fear and is a waste of time.

Some of the happiest times are spent outside enjoying nature, the quiet of walking in the forest, or seeing a new monument or site. If you don't go outside, you won't see it. When's the last time you walked in the rain? When is the last time you snow skied? You really don't like to be in the cold. But what about making a snowman, or going ice fishing, or cutting down a Christmas tree with the family?

I remember being in Anchorage and I wanted to cut a Christmas tree. So I got a permit and started on my trek for the perfect tree. The snow was about 24 inches deep and I could barely walk. It was a clear day and I had a golden retriever with me. The dog went in front of me, and suddenly we were both looking at a huge mama moose and her baby staring us in the eye. The dog normally would start barking, but this moose was big. I called the dog and walked backwards. The moose was getting ready to charge and protect her baby.

Chapter 26
People

******

'People are people," as they say. Different styles, shapes, races, colors and creeds are here. Each culture may have a different type of motivation and goals from you. It's your responsibility to figure out the motivation of each person. The way you do this is by asking questions.

It is important to understand what other people want. Your success lies in what motivates people especially if you are buying something or are in sales. Good sales people will know the personality types of each buyer. They will be able to sell our likes and dislikes. There are several books on this subject. Check them out, so you can get the scoop.

People's personalities and their abilities to understand what you are trying to convey will keep you in the "game". You must know what motivates other people. Study the topic of body language and what motivates people. Figure out their "buying" signs and you will be very successful.

Usually successful people are risk takers. They may have even gone bankrupt (a couple of times) and lost all their life savings. They have gone through divorce and lost their self-respect. The difference between winners and losers is that winners keep on trying. Winners make comebacks and accomplish goals.

To accomplish anything, you have to clear all obstacles from your thinking. Never think bad thoughts, especially if you are trying to accomplish something new. We all want to succeed, but do we? Do we just "get-by" or really put our all into projects? Do we accomplish our written goals or just do the least to get it done.

Evaluate yourself when you are finished with something new. You can't always blame "people" for your misfortunes. In essence it is YOU that controls what happens. Never, ever blame the place you're in or the people you come in contact with if things go wrong. Blame yourself for not figuring the correct path to take.

I would say 90 percent of the time; you're the one to blame. It's not the people you come in contact with. Be aware of these simple questions. Are you positive, have you done your homework, and are you COMMITTED to WIN?

Chapter 27

360 Degrees to Become Successful

******

At the time of this writing, my wife and I live in St. Augustine, Florida. This is a beautiful town called America's oldest city. I am back in Florida (who would have thought) because I miss my old job and especially my daughter, Ashley. I am a living, breathing example of a guy who is taking his own medicine and returning to what I know best. Nowhere in my wildest dreams did I think I would come back to Florida, but we kind of got a little dose of "island fever" living in Honolulu. When I tell people I moved here from Honolulu they look at me like, "Are you crazy?" I explain to them Hawaii was a great learning experience, but I wanted to come back for family and a little more driving experience.

You can't get in a car in Hawaii and drive to Texas. I made a 360 degree turn in my life and now will become truly successful because I am no longer living in the past!

Somebody told me long ago, "You made it once; you can make it again." I truly believe this.

Sometimes in your life you have to go 360 degrees and start over with WHAT WORKS BEST FOR YOU. If you go back, never be afraid or ashamed! You are a WINNER who will RISE AGAIN! Eliminate all objections if you come back to what you know. Don't start the project "half assed" as they say. Go like the winner you are!

Prepare for larger than life outcomes and never be ashamed going back. Your family and friends will understand IN TIME. Give them all the time they need and prove to them you made the right decision by your winning outcome and results.

You will have hecklers who tell you "Don't go." If you have the heart felt desire to succeed, you will succeed. You will become the winner they wished they were. You will become a positive influence on others by your actions.

Always remember to celebrate when you make the 'big" sale or win at a game. Always give a portion of your good fortune to someone who needs it more. Never pass by your brother or sister in need.

I certainly enjoyed writing this book. I hope in my heart you will get a few helpful hints to get you past the boredom and into winning like a champion. If you follow some of these simple tips, share them with other members of the family and THINK before you speak, you will become what you want to be.

In closing, I wish you the best success possible in this world! Keep very strong, focused and warmhearted with others. Drop me a line and tell me how you are doing. Other people would love to hear about your successes. May God bless you and give you all the abundance you deserve!

Index

******